Contemporary
earthenware

Arabic - with
charcoal
burner;
copper
and brass

1765
red stoneware

1776 silver

Contemporary
earthenware

Contemporary
stainless steel -
electric

to teachers and parents

This is a LADYBIRD LEADER book, one of a series specially produced to meet the very real need for carefully planned *first information books* that instantly attract enquiring minds and stimulate reluctant readers.

The subject matter and vocabulary have been selected with expert assistance, and the brief and simple text is printed in large, clear type.

Children's questions are anticipated and facts presented in a logical sequence. Where possible, the books show what happened in the past and what is relevant today.

Special artwork has been commissioned to set a standard rarely seen in books for this reading age and at this price.

Full colour illustrations are on all 48 pages to give maximum impact and provide the extra enrichment that is the aim of all Ladybird Leaders.

Acknowledgment

The publishers wish to acknowledge the help of the Nestlé Company Ltd in the preparation of this book.

A Ladybird Leader
coffee

by Michael Smith
with illustrations by David Palmer

Ladybird Books Ltd Loughborough 1977

The legend of Kaldi

A young Arabian goat-herd
noticed that his goats
were always more active
after they had eaten the berries
from certain trees.

They ran and jumped
just as though they were kids again.
He chewed the berries too
and felt just as lively.

He told his holy-man, who made
a brew of the berries in water
and gave it to his monks to drink.

It made them feel good
and helped them to stay awake
during the long hours of prayers.

The coffee tree

The berries had come
from the coffee tree,
which was growing wild.

A drink for the Ottoman army

The new drink soon became popular.
Many supply wagons of the army
of Suleiman the Magnificent
were loaded with coffee beans,
as his troops conquered lands
round the Mediterranean Sea
in the 16th century.

Coffee comes to Europe

By the middle of the 17th century coffee was being shipped from Arabia to European ports such as Marseilles.

The drink was thought to be able to cure certain illnesses.

Lloyd's coffee house in London

Edward Lloyd owned a coffee house where shipowners gathered to do business.

Groups such as artists and merchants each had a favourite coffee house.

Lloyd's coffee house
in Lombard Street, London

Early plantations

The demand for coffee beans
grew rapidly
and plantations of coffee trees
were started in Brazil
as early as 1723.

An early plantation in Brazil

Trade with the United States

The British put high taxes on tea,
which the Americans resented.

In 1773, dressed as Red Indians,
they boarded British cargo ships
and threw the tea in the water.

This was called the 'Boston Tea Party'

Then the Americans turned to coffee
which was much cheaper.

The Boston Tea Party

Modern plantations

Today there are coffee plantations
in many countries,
but all are in the tropics
because the trees need hot sun
and plenty of rain
at certain times of the year.

A modern coffee plantation estate

Coffee trees grow in hilly country

Plantations are found
in rolling, hilly country
often 450 metres above sea level.

The trees do best
in a rich volcanic soil.

Seedlings in a nursery

Trees are grown in nurseries
from the best seeds.

The young plants are shaded
from direct sunlight by taller trees.

They are transplanted
after about a year
when they are
about 45 centimetres high.

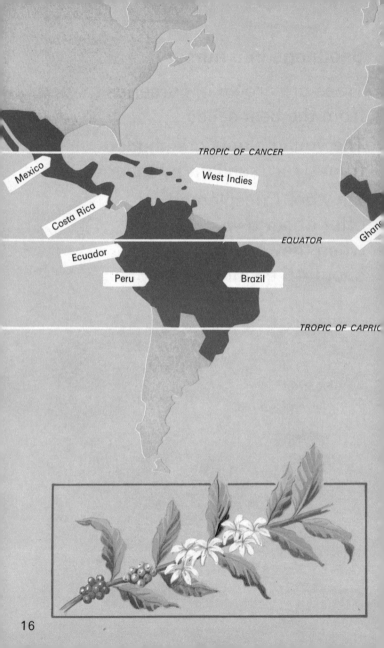

TROPIC OF CANCER

Mexico

West Indies

Costa Rica

EQUATOR

Ghana

Ecuador

Peru

Brazil

TROPIC OF CAPRICORN

16

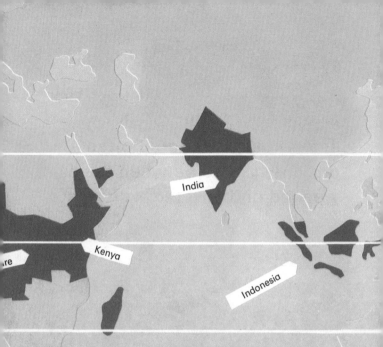

Where coffee grows

Coffee must have:

    127-228 cm of rain each year;
    a hot dry season
    in which to pick the beans;
    and rich well-drained soil.

Transplanting the seedlings

The seedlings are transplanted
to a permanent position.

They must be watered often
and the ground between the rows
weeded and covered with straw.

Careful cultivation

The young bushes are tended
carefully.

They have to be pruned,
and given fertilizer,
and sprayed to control
pests and diseases
which would harm them.

Flowers and fruit

Scented white flowers
appear on the branches
several times a year
amid the glossy green leaves.

At first the fruit is deep green,
but slowly the 'cherries' ripen
to yellow and then brilliant red.

The coffee 'cherry'

The bright red skin of the cherry
covers a sweet pulp
which has the two coffee beans
inside it.

Harvesting

In Africa and in Central America
each cherry is picked
and put into baskets.

The cherries ripen
at different times
so each is picked when ready.

In Brazil, the harvester
draws his hand along the branch
and the cherries fall onto sheets
or onto the ground.

The cherries are then collected
and *winnowed.*

This means that the cherries
are thrown into the air
so that the wind can blow away
the dust, leaves and twigs.

How the cherries are treated

The cherries are treated
in one of two ways
after they have been picked.

In Brazil they are spread
over huge drying floors
and are raked many times.

At night they are piled into heaps
and covered with sheets
to protect them from cold and damp.

When they are quite dry,
the beans are removed
from the skin and pulp by crushing,
which is done mechanically
by milling.

In Central America
and in East Africa,
the cherries are cleaned
in troughs of water.

Then they are put into reservoirs
where the pulp absorbs water.

This makes the pulp swell, so that most of it can be removed.

Later the beans ferment in tanks before being washed out clean and dried.

They are then graded.

Bagging the coffee

The clean 'green' beans
are now put into bags
ready for export.

Each full bag weighs 60 kilograms.

The fazenda

In Brazil the plantation
is called a *fazenda.*

It has houses for the workers
as well as sheds
for the machinery used.

Coffee estates in Kenya

In Kenya a coffee estate
may also have a church,
school and hospital.

The workers grow oranges as well as crops like beans and maize to eat.

An estate near Nakuru, Kenya

Coffee goes by train

The coffee bags have to be taken
from the fazenda
to the nearest port,
which may be
hundreds of kilometres away.

The port of Santos

Unloading at the Port of London

The load of coffee bags
is taken out of the cargo hold.
A tally man counts the sacks
as they are unloaded.

Taking a sample

Samples of coffee beans
are taken from different sacks.

A number of such samples
are sent to possible buyers.

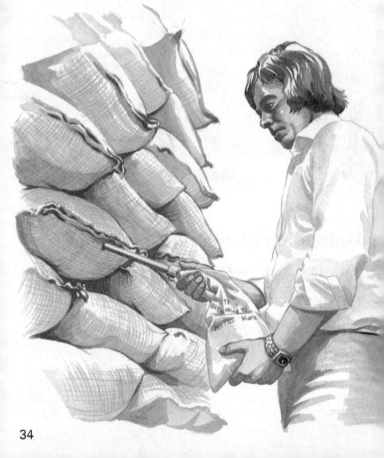

Roasting

Beans have little flavour
when harvested,
and have to be roasted
in metal cylinders
heated by gas or electricity.

Have you passed a shop
where beans are being roasted?

Different types of coffee

Coffee beans from different parts
of the world
have different flavours.

People choose the one they like best,
or a blend of several types.

Grinding

There are different ways
of making coffee too.

First the beans must be ground,
either at the shop
or in a grinder in the kitchen.

Freshly-ground beans
give the best flavour.

Making coffee

Boiling water can be poured
over the ground coffee
and left to stand for four minutes.

Some people use a percolator.

Serving coffee

Coffee can be served black
or with heated milk,
or with cream.

Beakers or cups?

Coffee drunk during the day
is best served
in a large cup or pottery beaker.

For coffee after dinner,
special small cups may be used.

Coffee sets can be very attractive.

Sweetening coffee

Demerara, a coarse brown sugar,
is often used,
because it adds a special flavour.
Sometimes you see
pretty coloured coffee sugar.

Iced coffee

Coffee can also be enjoyed cold.

The coffee and the milk
are chilled separately
in the refrigerator.

They are then mixed
and poured over ice cubes.

Instant coffee

Sometimes there isn't time
to make ground coffee,
so instant coffees can be bought
which need only to have
hot milk and water added.

How instant coffee is produced

The manufacturers of instant coffees start by brewing ground coffee.

Then the water is removed, leaving a pure coffee powder.

Beans are blended to produce nearly as many different flavours in instant coffees as in ground coffees.

Cooking with coffee

Instant coffees can also
be used in cooking
to flavour cakes, icecream
and other sweet things.

Blending is a skilled task

Since different flavours of coffee
are popular in different countries,
blending is done by experts
in each country
where coffee is drunk.

Vending machines

At stations and in factories,
hospitals and other places
where people need to be able
to buy a drink at any time,
you will see vending machines
which will serve coffee
or other drinks.

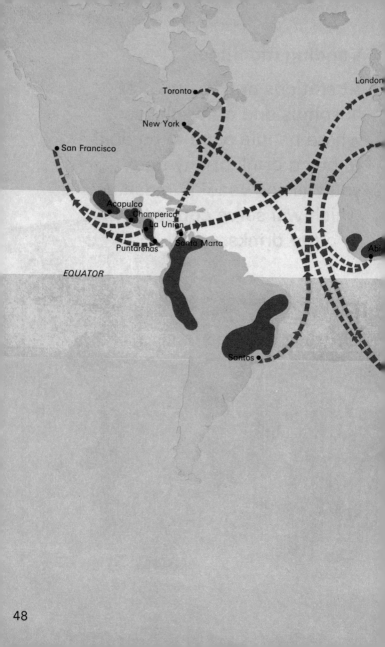

EQUATOR

London

Toronto

New York

San Francisco

Acapulco
Champerico
La Union
Puntarenas
Santa Marta

Abi

Santos

The export of coffee

Coffee travels to ports throughout the world.

Coffee is served

Coffee is enjoyed
in submarines deep in the ocean
or in airliners high in the air.

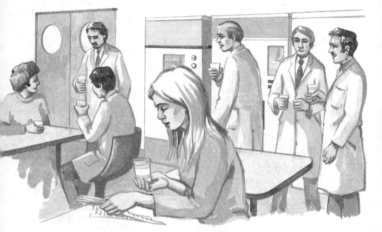

When we work
and when we play
coffee gives us new vigour.

Index